Modern World Religions

Buddhism

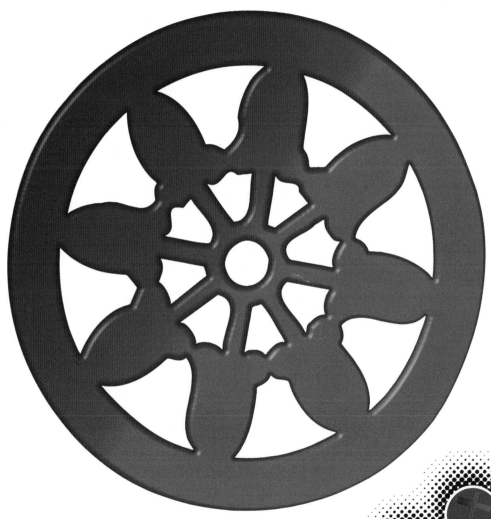

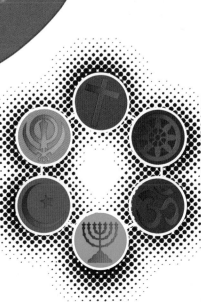

Cavan Wood

Heinemann

To my wife Sarah, for her love and support

Heinemann Educational Publishers
Halley Court, Jordan Hill, Oxford, OX2 8EJ
Part of Harcourt Education

Heinemann is the registered trademark of Harcourt Education Limited

First published in 2002

06
10 9 8 7 6 5

British Library Cataloguing in Publication Data
A catalogue record for this book is available from the British Library

10-digit ISBN: 0 435 33603 7
13-digit ISBN: 978 0 435 33603 5

Picture research by Jennifer Johnson
Typeset by Artistix, Thame, Oxon
Printed and bound in Spain by Edelvives

Acknowledgements

The publishers would like to thank the following for permission to use photographs: AKG London/Gilles Mermet, p. 7; Andes Press Agency/C & D Hill, pp. 6 and 37 (bottom); Andes Press Agency/Carlos Reyes Manzo, pp. 16, 18, 19, 27 (top), 30, 47 and 57; Robin Bath, pp. 3, 8, 23 (top), 24, 25, 27 (bottom), 31 (middle and right), 38 and 58; Camerapress/Benoit Gysembergh, p. 59; Christine Osborne Pictures, pp. 10, 29, 34, 37 (top), 46, 48 (bottom), 50 and 52; Christine Osborne Pictures/Nick Dawson, p. 39; Christine Osborne/P Kapoor, p. 23 (bottom); Christine Osborne Pictures/S A Molton, p. 31 (left); Circa Photo Library/William Holtby, pp. 26, 36 and 40; Hutchison Library/Jon Burbank, p. 4 (bottom); Hutchison Library/Jeremy Horner, p. 48 (top); Karuna Trust, p. 53; Ann & Bury Peerless, p. 4 (top); Angela Walker, p. 41.

The publishers have made every effort to contact copyright holders. However, if any material has been incorrectly acknowledged, the publishers would be pleased to correct this at the earliest opportunity.

Websites

Links to appropriate websites are given throughout the book. Although these were up-to-date at the time of writing, it is essential for teachers to preview these sites before using them with pupils. This will ensure that the web address (URL) is still accurate and the content is suitable for your needs. We suggest that you bookmark useful sites and consider enabling pupils to access them through the school intranet. We are bringing this to your attention as we are aware of legitimate sites being appropriated illegally by people wanting to distribute unsuitable and offensive material. We strongly advise you to purchase suitable screening software so that pupils are protected from unsuitable sites and their material. If you do find that the links given no longer work, or the content is unsuitable, please let us know. Details of changes will be posted on our website.

Tel: 01865 888058   www.heinemann.co.uk

Contents

Introduction

In this section you will:

● learn about the Buddhist religion and its place in a multicultural society

● reflect on how religions influence the world we know.

A religion without God?

You might think that in order for something to be a religion, then you have to believe in God. **Buddhism** is a religion, yet Buddhists do not have to believe in a god. Most Buddhists would say that they are agnostic about whether or not a god exists.

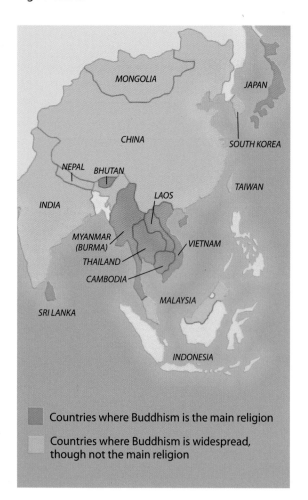

Countries where Buddhism is the main religion

Countries where Buddhism is widespread, though not the main religion

Countries where Buddhism is the main religion today

Although Buddhism does not believe in a god, it does have many other features that you find in a religion. It has ideas about life and death, holy books, festivals, religious leaders, prayer, meditation and special ceremonies to mark events such as birth, marriage and death.

Buddhism began with the birth of **Siddhartha Gautama** in India in 563 BCE. About thirty-five years later, he became known as the **Buddha** and travelled through India until his death in 483 BCE.

The religion he started soon spread across the neighbouring countries such as Sri Lanka, Tibet and Nepal. The larger countries such as Japan, China and Korea were converted to Buddhism.

As you can see from the map, Buddhism isn't limited to Asia. When the British Empire had control of India, many people travelled to the region and learned about the traditions there. Other travellers to Japan and China returned to Victorian Britain to tell about the religion of the Buddha.

In the early years of the twentieth century, The Buddhist Society was founded in London to explain and promote Buddhism in the UK. One member was Christmas Humphreys, who was to become a very famous barrister and later a judge.

In the 1960s, Buddhism became more popular in the West. Many young people thought that Buddhist pacifist principles (anti-war), vegetarianism and stress on humans finding out the truth for themselves, rather than looking for the solutions from a god, fitted with their beliefs. Another important Buddhist belief is that of re-birth, that human beings and all other life-forms go through many lifetimes until they reach the ultimate state of happiness, **nirvana**.

Musicians such as The Beatles quoted from Buddhist books such as the Tibetan *Book of the Dead*. Artists found inspiration from the **mandalas** and other Buddhist pictures.

An example of Buddhist art

Many other young people found out about Buddhism when they were serving in Vietnam. The film director Oliver Stone became a Buddhist while serving there.

Buddhism has also become popular with many other people. They include the rock singers Tina Turner and musician Suzanne Vega, and film stars Richard Gere and Keanu Reeves.

Films such as *Kundun*, *Little Buddha* and *Seven Years in Tibet* have shown that the interest in Buddhism continues to grow.

The **Dalai Lama**, the spiritual and political leader of Tibet is a well-known Buddhist leader. He was forced into exile in India following the Chinese invasion of Tibet in the 1950s.

In Burma, the political leader and Buddhist, Aung San Suu Kyi has become an internationally known figure for standing up against a military government that seized power when her party had won a majority in an election.

Buddhism's teachings about re-birth, harmlessness (often shown by many Buddhists being vegetarians), non-violence and using meditation to find a way to truth have become popular with many people as they seem to be an alternative to what they were brought up to believe.

Learning about religion

❶ Write down some of the ideas that have been attractive to people when they have thought about Buddhism. Which might attract you to Buddhism? Give reasons.

❷ Look at the map. Which country has the largest population of Buddhists? Which has the least?

❸ 'If it doesn't believe in God, it isn't really a religion.' How might a Buddhist answer this? What do you think? Give reasons for your answers.

Learning from religion

❶ Many Buddhists are vegetarians. Organize a class debate to look at the pluses and minuses of being a vegetarian.

❷ 'Buddhism is 2,500 years old and irrelevant.' Discuss this statement. How do you think a Buddhist would respond?

❸ Using the Internet, research a Buddhist country and prepare a talk about the country, showing how Buddhism has affected it.

The birth of the Buddha

In this section you will:

● learn about the birth stories told about the **Buddha** and their symbolic meanings

● reflect on the importance of birth and its value in giving meaning.

Queen Mayadevi's dream

Queen Mayadevi's dream

Some Buddhists believe that the Buddha had existed in a heavenly realm before he came to earth. They believe he also had lived through several thousand other lifetimes – both animal and human – before he was born.

In the country of the Sakyas (a tribe who lived in areas that we call India and Nepal today) there lived a King called Suddhodana who was married to Queen Mayadevi. The Queen was very beautiful, fearless and a good person. She told her husband of her great feelings of joy and peace one evening. She asked him to refrain from sexual intercourse for a while.

The Queen returned to her room and fell asleep. As she slept that night, she had a dream of a six-tusked white elephant, who had a head the colour of rubies. This was a sign that Buddha himself had left heaven and was entering the world through her womb.

Explaining the dream

In the morning, the Queen told the King that she had had a dream. The King decided to summon eight holy men to explain the dream.

They told him that the dream was a good sign. It meant that the baby in the womb would either be a great emperor or a great holy man.

Lumbini Grove today

The birth of the Buddha

The Queen and the King went to the wood of **Lumbini Grove** at the time the birth was expected. The Queen stepped from her chariot, followed by dancers and musicians.

She strolled until she was beneath the shade of a sala tree. The tree bent down and the Queen took hold of a bending branch. As she looked into the sky, she saw the lucky stars of Pushya shining very brightly, a sign that great things were to happen.

As she stood there, the baby Buddha was born from her right side. Without any help, the child walked seven steps to the North, then the South, then the East and then the West. At every step, a **lotus flower** sprang from the ground. His limbs shone as bright as gold. He seemed to beam a light to all those around him.

The child spoke, 'No further births will I have to suffer, for this will be my last body. Now shall I destroy and pluck out the roots of the sorrow that is caused by the wheel of birth, life and death.'

When the King was told of the child's birth, he thought long and hard about what the boy should be called. He said, 'I shall call him **Siddhartha**, meaning "Perfect Fulfilment" because on the day of his birth all things were done to perfection.'

Seven days after his birth, Queen Mayadevi died. Eventually, the King married Mayadevi's sister, Mahapajapah, who cared for Siddhartha as if she were his real mother.

A wise man called Asita came to see the baby and found 32 marks that showed the boy would lead people to great truth. Asita began to cry, for he realized that he would not live long enough to see the child become the man who would teach people so many truths.

The King grew afraid of the talk of priests and other holy people and decided to bring the boy up in such a way that he would not leave the palace for the wandering, religious life of a monk.

Learning about religion

❶ Make a list of things that happen in the birth story of the Buddha in one column and those things that happen in the birth stories of Jesus in the other. What do they have in common? What is different? Use the stories in Matthew 1 and 2 and in Luke 1 and 2 in the New Testament to help you. What do the two stories tell you about the beliefs people have about the Buddha and Jesus?

❷ Many Buddhists are not sure if the story of Buddha's birth happened as the story says, but they still think it is important. What might this story tell you about beliefs people have about the Buddha?

❸ Produce a newspaper called 'Palace News', written by a palace reporter about the birth of the Buddha. Show two points of view about the event.

Learning from religion

❶ Many religions have stories with important dreams in them. Can you remember an important dream you have had or one that someone had which they thought was important to them? Why did you/they think it was important?

❷ If you had a child, what things might you think about when trying to choose a name and why?

❸ 'The stories about the birth of the Buddha are so unbelievable that they can teach us nothing of use for today.' How might a Buddhist respond to this? What do you think?

The discontented prince

In this section you will:

● learn how Prince **Siddhartha** became discontented with the life he was living and the importance he came to attach to a search for meaning and truth

● think about what are the most important questions in life for yourself.

Chained to unhappiness

Prince **Siddhartha** grew up in a loving, happy environment. His father gave him his own palace, with all the servants he could ever need. He had all his needs attended to.

When he was a young man, he once protected a swan from an arrow let loose from a bow by one of his friends. It is a story still told today not only to show how much he cared for the bird, but also as a way of saying that he knew what unhappiness could mean.

Yet his father the King went to great lengths to stop his son from knowing about pain. Perhaps the King still felt the pain of having lost his wife so soon after the birth of his son. Whatever was the cause, the King made sure that any servants who were ill, old or died were removed so that Siddhartha would not see them.

The young Prince Siddhartha

Perhaps if he saw these people, Siddhartha might well ask questions that would lead him to the religious life that the King was afraid that his son might follow.

So Siddhartha lived. He was banned from going into the city, in case he should see the truth of life.

Siddhartha fell in love with a beautiful princess called **Yashodahra**. All seemed perfect, especially when their first son was born. But Prince Siddhartha called him '**Rahula**', which means 'chain', a sign that he was very unhappy.

Visits to the city

One day, Siddhartha was talking to **Channa**, the man who drove the King's chariot. He asked him to take him into the city. Channa refused, but Siddhartha insisted, and eventually the chariot driver took him there.

On his first visit, Siddhartha saw an old man, leaning almost bent double on a stick. He asked what was wrong with him.

'He is old,' said Channa. 'One day, we shall all be like him, both princes and ordinary people.'

On a second visit to the city, Siddhartha saw an ill man lying on the side of the road. Channa told him that illness happened to all, a reality that none could escape from.

Siddhartha was confused – why had his father hidden these truths of existence from him? On a third visit, he saw a dead man, lying and decaying by the side of the road. Channa told him that all people would die.

Siddhartha returned to the palace, confused and wanting answers. On a fourth journey to the city, Siddhartha saw a bald man, carrying a bowl and dressed only in a simple robe. He asked Channa who this man was. Channa told him that this was a holy man, an ascetic, who had given up everything for the cause of truth.

Siddhartha cuts off his hair before his enlightenment

Siddhartha decided that he must leave the palace in order to get to the truth. Early one morning, when everyone in the palace had fallen into a deep sleep, Siddhartha awoke and woke Channa, whom he ordered to take him to the forest where the holy men lived.

As he dismounted from the chariot at the edge of the wood, Siddhartha gave his princely cloak to Channa. Taking a knife, he cut off his ponytail. Now he would begin his search for truth with the holy men.

Learning about religion

❶ Was Siddhartha's father being loving in trying to protect him from the outside world? Give reasons for your answer, showing that you have thought about it from more than one point of view.

❷ Buddhists believe that Siddhartha saw visions of the old, the ill, the dead and the holy man rather than actually see them in the flesh. Does it make any difference if he saw them in his mind or in the flesh?

❸ Write Siddhartha's diary, showing how he moved from a discontented prince to a seeker after truth in the forest.

Learning from religion

❶ How could someone like Siddhartha who had everything he needed be so unhappy?

❷ Siddhartha left home as he wanted to answer the big questions. What are the most important questions to you? Can they all be answered or not?

❸ 'It wasn't fair of Siddhartha to leave his family behind. He was being selfish.' How might a Buddhist reply to this? What do you think?

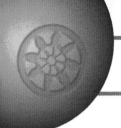

The enlightenment of the Buddha

The enlightened Buddha

In this section you will:

- understand the importance of the **enlightenment** of the **Buddha** to Buddhists
- reflect on those moments when we change and grow as people.

A flash of inspiration

The story goes that when the scientist Isaac Newton sat under an apple tree, an apple fell off and made him realize that gravity was at work.

Alexander Fleming noticed that some mould on bread killed bacteria and, as a result of his work, we now have penicillin. Scientists can often be inspired to suddenly see things that no-one else has ever noticed.

Religious people have often regarded sudden flashes of inspiration as important, though they often say you may need to wait years to receive them!

Siddhartha leaves the holy men

After he left the palace, **Siddhartha** joined a group of holy men who practised **asceticism**. This is the belief that if you deny your body things, you can get to know the truth about the world. Siddhartha slept on thorns, ate mud and at one point tried to live on no more than one grain of rice a day.

One day, as he was meditating, he heard a passing musician tell a pupil, 'If the strings are too tight, they will break and not play. If they are too slack, they also will not play.'

Siddhartha realized that he would not find the truth either living the life of pleasure that he had as a prince or by denying himself as he had done so living with the holy men. The truth would lie between the two opposites, what he was later to call the **Middle Way**.

Siddhartha went to the river and there a local girl gave him a drink. He accepted her offer of food. The holy men were appalled and would not listen to him, seeing him as a traitor.

Siddhartha becomes the Buddha

Siddhartha left the holy men and went to a place called **Bodh Gaya**. He decided to sit under a bodhi tree, waiting there until he had reached full understanding of the big questions in life.

THE MIDDLE WAY

The Middle Way lies between pain and pleasure

According to Buddhists, a devil figure called **Mara** tried to keep him from the truth. First Mara sent his daughters to try to keep him from his quest. These daughters were human incarnations of lust, ignorance and greed. When Siddhartha ignored them, Mara made him believe firstly that he was in the middle of a great storm and then that he was being attacked by a great army. But still Siddhartha continued to meditate.

Finally, Mara appeared as the exact image of Siddhartha. But Siddhartha saw through the deception and he rested from these attacks.

During the night that followed, Siddhartha came to understand the other lives he had had. He also realized the nature of suffering and that freedom from suffering could be found. The truth of suffering he identified in what he called the **Four Noble Truths** and the **Eightfold Path**, which he saw as a path to a way that gives people freedom or liberation.

He was no longer Siddhartha but the Buddha. 'Buddha' means 'the enlightened or awoken one'. Siddhartha had 'woken up' to what life was really about.

Learning about religion

❶ Draw a diagram to explain the idea of the Middle Way.

❷ Why do you think Mara tried to stop Siddhartha becoming the Buddha?

❸ 'The Buddha's experiences are very helpful to those who seek enlightenment today.' Why might this be so?

Learning from religion

❶ How might the Middle Way be relevant today, even if you aren't a Buddhist?

❷ Why do you think so many religious people think there must be some kind of devil figure?

❸ Are ideas like the Devil a way of avoiding responsibility for our own bad choices? What do you think? Give reasons for your answers.

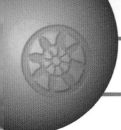

The death of the Buddha

In this section you will:

- find out about the later life and death of the **Buddha**
- think about the questions the Buddha's life raises for us now.

The Buddha as a teacher

For 45 years, the Buddha travelled the length of India teaching his ideas. He gathered a group of disciples, who eventually included the holy men who had once rejected him, his son **Rahula** and the man who succeeded him, **Ananda**.

The story of Kisagami

'We die all the time, from moment to moment and what is really there is a perpetual succession of extremely shortlived events.'

Edward Conze

In the above quote, Conze means that over seven years, every cell in your body dies and is replaced by another. There is a very real sense in which we are dying all the time and we need to face up to this.

One day, an unhappy woman called **Kisagami** came to the Buddha. Her child had recently died and, in her shock, she carried him around. She came to the Buddha, asking that he perform a miracle and cure the child.

The Buddha and his disciples

The Buddha realized that she had not really accepted the death of the child and so he set her a task to make her come to terms with the reality.

'Go and collect mustard seeds from every house where death has not visited and then return with them and I will help you.'

Kisagami travelled and knocked on every door she could. But the answer was always the same – many people had died over the years in each of the houses she visited.

She returned to the Buddha and quietly lay the body of her child at his feet.

She looked at him with tears in her eyes and said, 'Now I realize that I am not alone in my grief and that all will be touched by death.'

The Buddha told her that she must now bury her child. From that day on, Kisagami became a Buddhist.

The death of the Buddha

The Buddha was 80 years old when the time came for him to die. According to Buddhist belief, he hinted to his assistant Ananda that he would soon die but Ananda did not realize.

On a visit to a follower called **Chunda**, Buddha ate something which gave him food poisoning (in all probability a mushroom).

The Buddha had his disciples come to stay at **Kusingara**, where he entered into **nirvana** at the time of his death.

The funeral pyre was not lit until the Malian monks were able to reach the scene. The passing of the Buddha was greeted with music, dancing and joy – he had achieved his goal and had helped so many other people to understand the truth. To be sad seemed to be wrong in some ways.

In his teaching, the Buddha had said that, 'Every moment you are born, decay and die but we continue and are reborn elsewhere.'

After the funeral fire died down, the traditional stories tell us that there were 84,000 relics of the Buddha left. These have been preserved in Buddhist buildings across Asia. These buildings include a stupa in the city of Kandy in Sri Lanka. This is said to contain one of the Buddha's teeth (see pages 36–7).

Learning about religion

❶ Was the Buddha cruel or wise in the way he dealt with Kisagami's grief at her dead son?

❷ Write an obituary for the Buddha, as if you were writing for a paper that believed in his teachings.

❸ Write a poem about the story of Kisagami.

Learning from religion

❶ 'True Buddhism died with the death of the Buddha.' Do you agree?

❷ Is thinking about death a morbid thing to do? Give reasons for your answer.

❸ What could you do to try to ensure that people remember you as you would like to be remembered? You might like to write a short obituary for yourself.

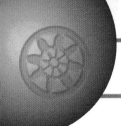

Buddhist teaching on suffering

In this section you will:

● learn about the importance of the **Four Noble Truths** and the **Eightfold Path** to Buddhists

● reflect on how to deal with the problem of suffering.

The Buddha's teaching

The **Buddha** taught that there were Four Noble Truths.

1. Old age, sickness and death will happen to us all – we all suffer.

2. Suffering comes about from wanting (desire).

3. Non-attachment is freedom.

4. Use your skills and follow the Eightfold Path.

The Buddha wanted people to realize the truths about life. He thought that the desires, the longings people have to own things, to have certain relationships or any other sorts of longings would only lead to pain, because they cannot be permanent.

When the Buddha said that there was no such thing as a self, he was saying that humans are a continuous process of different parts and events that come together for a time. A Buddhist called **Nagasena** once wrote that the self was a bit like a chariot. A chariot is made up of parts such as a wheel or an axle but there is no such thing as a chariot, as it is made up from parts. What we call a self is made up of things such as love, anger, humour, wisdom and other qualities which will become separated at death, rather like seeds of a dandelion becoming separated by the wind. What we need, he said, is to realize that we are believing an illusion and hoping that we are always going to remain the same.

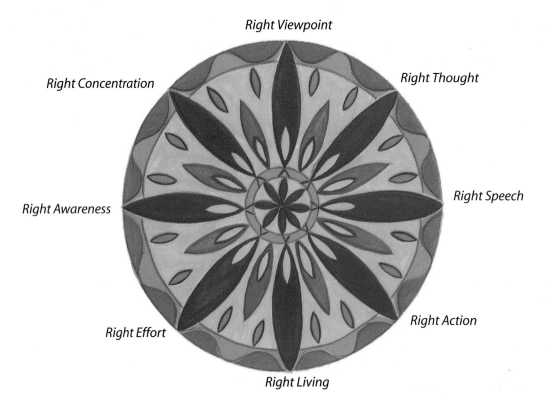

The Eightfold Path

By following the noble **Eightfold Path**, Buddhists believe they can find a way to end suffering and see beyond the illusion.

The Eightfold Path is not eight individual steps, but rather a way that needs to be taken together. The eight steps are:

1. Right Understanding: you must realize the truths that the Buddha has given you.

2. Right Intention: if you follow the path, you must always make sure that you do all of these things for the right reasons.

3. Right Speech: you need to speak in a way that does not keep dwelling on yourself. You need to speak to others in a way that shows respect, and which is harmless and avoids rudeness or dishonesty.

4. Right Action: you must live your life in such a way that you follow the teachings of the Buddha by attempting to keep the **Five Moral Precepts**.

5. Right Livelihood: it is very important that you choose a job that stops you from being arrogant or leading you to violence. Most Buddhists would avoid professions such as butchery or the armed forces because they would have to use violence in order to do their job.

6. Right Effort: if you are using **meditation** and making sure that you do the right things, then you will not be attached to the outcomes of effort.

7. Right Mindfulness: through meditation you become aware of all that you do in thought, speech and action.

8. Right Concentration: you need to be free of worry, anxiety and envy in order to think clearly.

Buddhists also believe they should develop four essential qualities: metta (loving kindness), karuna (compassion), mudita (sympathetic joy) and upekkah (see page 29).

Learning about religion

1. Draw a diagram to show the third part of the Noble Truths.

2. Discuss which of the Four Noble Truths and the Eightfold Path are the most difficult to believe or to practise.

3. 'The Eightfold Path is really a set of disguised rules.' What would the Buddha have thought about this?

Learning from religion

1. 'Desire leads to pain.' Do you believe this is true? Give reasons for your answer, showing that you have thought about more than one point of view. Also, remember that there are many different ways to understand pain.

2. 'It would be impossible for anyone to fully live out the idea of Right Speech.' What do you think? Give reasons for your answers.

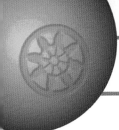

Five Moral Precepts

Good intentions

Imagine you had a friend who always let you down. We think that it is very important to always keep our promises. It seems that people who cannot keep their promises in small things will not be able to keep their word on big things. The Buddha called his followers to follow five intentions to live a good life. These are called the Five Moral Precepts.

Avoid taking what is not given

Five intentions

The Buddha was not like other religious leaders in that he made suggestions based on his own experience and understanding rather than making rules which told his followers what to do.

What were his five suggestions?

1. **To avoid taking life**. This intention was to extend to both animal and human life, so many Buddhists are vegetarians and are pacifists. Many Buddhists would say that this promise also means that they should try to be aware of the implications of abortion and euthanasia. There may be occasions where taking a life is unavoidable, but the intention not to cause harm is the main focus. Buddhists believe in **ahimsa**, which means that no violence should be committed if at all possible.

2. **To avoid taking what is not given**. This is an intention to avoid stealing from others. Some Buddhists say that this does not just refer to stealing possessions. It could mean stealing from someone else's ideas or reputation by claiming to have done something when you have not, perhaps taking the glory for something you should not.

3. **To avoid sexual misconduct**. Buddhists believe that they should live their lives in ways that do not hurt other people. As sex is such an important area, they believe that it is important that it takes place in committed relationships. For some, this will mean that they get married, but other Buddhists, especially in countries such as the UK and the USA, argue that what matters is being committed to each other. So you may well live with someone in a heterosexual or homosexual relationship.

Avoid speaking falsely and gossiping

4. **To avoid speaking falsely**. This intention includes not lying, not gossiping or deliberately trying to wound someone by words. Buddhists believe that people should always try to tell each other the truth but in a respectful way. People should always listen to others' points of view. This intention also encourages Buddhists not to speak too much or too loudly.

5. **To avoid drink and drugs that can cloud the mind**. Buddhists believe that it is unskilful to get drunk. Similarly, they are not against using drugs for medical reasons, but they do not feel that taking drugs to get a high is helpful to them because they feel it is a way to avoid reality rather than face it. The Buddha said that a being with pain helps to release pain – this means that we can help and support each other.

The Buddha believed that if people kept these promises, they would be able to grow in wisdom and understanding of what is **skilful**, or right, and what is lacking in skill, or that which is likely to cause suffering. The Buddha also believed that if they followed these promises, they would develop **karuna**, that is a compassionate love for all others.

Learning about religion

1. Write a diary of a school pupil your age who is trying to live by the Five Moral Precepts.

2. What do ahimsa and karuna mean? How easy are these qualities to follow?

3. 'The Buddha's moral precepts are too difficult to live by.' What would a Buddhist say? Arrange the Five Moral Precepts in the order you consider to be most important.

Learning from religion

1. How could you avoid speaking falsely?

2. Design a collage to explain the Five Moral Precepts to a group of primary age children.

Nirvana, karma and rebirth

In this section you will:

● learn about **nirvana**, **karma** and rebirth which are very important ideas to Buddhists

● reflect on the cause and consequences of your actions, as well as the universal interest in the idea of a paradise.

The promise of a paradise

Human beings have often longed to find a place where they can live good lives and where all things will be easy. Humans have dreamed of finding a paradise where they will be able to live freely.

Buddhists believe that the ultimate goal is to reach nirvana. This is not really a place, but a state of being. It is a state of being reached when we have overcome the dream of having a self and have become one with the universe.

Rebirth

Buddhists believe that we are trapped on a **wheel of life**. They believe that we will be reborn many times in order to give us the opportunity to reach nirvana, which is freedom from suffering or clinging to being.

Buddhists believe that we do not know it, but that we may be reborn as humans or as animals or even as plants. Sometimes, a particular rebirth might be for a reason, for example to teach us a particular quality – a very impatient person may well be reborn as a tree as a way to teach them to be patient!

When you are reborn as a human being, you should not waste the opportunity this gives you, because it is only as a human being that you will be able to reach **enlightenment**. Only human beings have the mental capacity to reach enlightenment.

Nirvana is the spiritual equivalent of paradise

The **Buddha** once said that the chances of being reborn as a human being were the same as those of a blind turtle being able to swim through a ring in a 100 years in a vast ocean.

What goes around, comes around

Have you ever done something and seen the consequences come back on you? Perhaps you have said something unpleasant about someone else and they have found out, resulting in an argument between you. Or perhaps you have tried to get out of doing a piece of work, only to see yourself being kept in detention for it.

Or there again, you might have had the satisfaction of doing something good for someone else and seeing them benefit from your actions.

Buddhists believe that the rebirths that arise are a result of the karma we have. Karma is the idea that every action has a reaction. If people do good, then good will follow. If people choose to do evil, then evil will follow – or as you sow so you will reap. The results of karma can be experienced in the present lifetime, even day by day.

In **Buddhism**, karma can go from one lifetime to another and therefore it is vital that people try to live the best life they can, as they will often have the bad karma of previous lifetimes to deal with. Karma will determine whether people reach enlightenment or have to live 1000 lifetimes of a lesser animal in order to get to the truth.

Karma does not just work for individuals but can also have an effect on the whole nation or the whole planet. Buddhists talk about collective karma, when the consequences of actions taken by whole countries can often change things. For example, Buddhists would argue that the way rich nations treat the poorer nations of the world may well affect the karma of a whole country or a group such as the United Nations.

The wheel of life

Learning about religion

❶ What do Buddhists mean by 'nirvana'?

❷ Design a wall display to explain re-birth and karma.

❸ Organize a class discussion, 'This house believes in re-birth'. Make sure you have covered points for and against the motion.

Learning from religion

❶ Do you agree that all actions have consequences? Explain your views.

❷ Write a story about someone who thinks they have been born before.

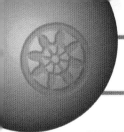

The Three Refuges

A person to follow

Various different people can help us in different ways. A police officer might warn us if there are traffic problems ahead. A tour guide will help get us to the destination we want to visit on holiday. A team coach will give us advice and support in sporting activities.

Buddhists believe in what they call the Three Refuges (sometimes also called the Three Jewels). These refuges are designed to help them, but Buddhists believe these supports exist within a person.

The first of the Three Refuges is remembered in the vow:

'I go to the Buddha for refuge.'

The symbol for the Three Refuges

To be a Buddha is to be a being who is awake to the way the world is, who is wise and can see clearly. Buddhists believe that people can use their own experiences to see clearly and throw light onto a situation. Experience can show clearer pathways if people reflect on the pathways they have used and know. Insight is people's own gut feeling or inner voice of wisdom that they trust. Refuge can be found in the confidence that these feelings bring.

The Dharma

The second of the Three Refuges is:

'I go to the Dharma for refuge.'

The Dharma is the Buddhist name for the teaching of the Buddha, which can be found in scriptures such as the **Pali Canon**. The word 'dharma' literally means 'universal truth', a truth that needs to be responded to and lived out in practice.

Buddhists may consult specially trained teachers of the scriptures, such as monks, to understand all the truth about what the Buddha taught. They may also use meditation to find it for themselves.

Some Buddhists, such as those who follow Zen Buddhism, often have teachers who make wise statements and tell stories in order to help them to understand the Dharma.

Reading the Dharma

We all have a need to belong to a group

The need to belong

It is very important that we all have a sense of belonging. We need to belong to groups in order to feel secure. Families and friends can help us out and stick by us when we feel in trouble or unloved.

The third of the Three Refuges is:

'I go to the Sangha for refuge.'

For some Buddhists, the word 'sangha' refers to those Buddhists who live as monks and nuns. However, most Buddhists believe that the Sangha is the name that should be given to anyone who belongs to a local **vihara** or temple.

It is very important for Buddhists to belong to a Sangha because this enables them to take a fully active part in the festivals of their religion. It enables them to share their insights and understandings gained through meditation and prayer, as well as share problems they face. The Sangha is a community of like-minded spiritual friends, trying to support and encourage each other in the development of their faith.

Learning about religion

❶ Design a leaflet to explain the importance of the three refuges to Buddhists.

❷ 'All three parts of the three refuges are as important as the other.' What would a Buddhist say? Do you agree?

❸ 'You could be a good Buddhist without joining a group.' What would a Buddhist say to this?

Learning from religion

❶ What do people try to use to make themselves happy and secure?

❷ Should you ever do anything from a sense of gratitude? If so, what?

❸ What would you say are the three most important things in your life? Explain your selection.

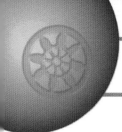

Types of Buddhism

In this section you will:

- learn about the similarities and differences between the two types of **Buddhism**
- reflect on why differences develop within groups.

Witness to a crime

Imagine a crime had been committed. When it came to a trial, the witnesses might not agree about many of the details. They might disagree about the facts of what had happened, why things happened, in what order they occurred and what they mean!

Yet in a court of law, it might still be possible to convict someone of a crime, even if all the witnesses do not agree on all the key parts. They may differ, but together they can give you enough detail to develop a picture of the truth.

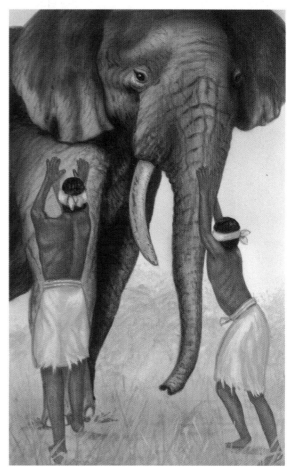

The blind men and the elephant

Blind men and elephants

A famous Buddhist story tells of a king who asked a group of blind men to each feel a part of an elephant and describe what they thought an elephant was like. The one who held the trunk thought it was like a snake, the one who touched the leg thought it was like a tree trunk and so on. They did not accurately define the truth by themselves, yet their poetic descriptions of the elephant had a certain truth.

Many Buddhists would say that the different types of Buddhism can never by themselves get to the whole truth, but that they are pointers in the general direction of the truth.

A witness to a crime can be important

Theravada Buddhism

'**Theravada**' means 'the teaching of the elders'. Theravada Buddhism bases its teachings on the material in the **Pali Canon** (the original text).

Theravada Buddhists believe that the **Buddha** was only a man, not superhuman.

Theravada Buddhists believe that the religious life is more easily available to those who live as monks and nuns who are supported in their practice by the **Sangha**. They stress that merit can be achieved by trying to follow the Six Perfections:

1. morality (**sila**)
2. generosity (**dana**)
3. patience (**kshanti**)
4. energy (**virya**)
5. concentration (**dhyana**)
6. wisdom (**prajna**).

Mahayana Buddhism

Mahayana Buddhism began in the first century BCE. It is most popular in countries such as Korea, Tibet and China.

Mahayana Buddhists believe that all people can become Buddhas. They believe that the Buddha was a special figure.

They talk of the Buddha as having three bodies:

1. transformation body – the body he had when he was alive
2. enjoyment body – the body with which he can visit people in visions today
3. thought body – the body in which he will appear in a future time.

Mahayana Buddhists also stress the importance of **Bodhisattvas**, 'the Buddhas to be', who decided not to stay back and continue to be reborn in this world or exist in another realm in order to help lead us to the truth.

There are other types of Buddhism too. Nichiren Shoshu is named after a thirteenth-century monk called Nichiren Daishonin. Nichiren Daishonin believed that he completed the Buddha's message. His followers believe that they can fulfil their needs through chanting.

Learning about religion

1. What do you think the Buddha would say about there being different types of Buddhist? Give your reasons.

2. Find out in depth about one of the Theravada and one of the Mahayana countries. Use the Internet to help you in this research.

3. Would the Buddha have wanted to be worshipped? Give evidence to support your answer.

Learning from religion

1. How can people who are committed to different beliefs live alongside one another in harmony?

2. 'Religion says it wants to bring people together, it always tears them apart.' Organize a class debate on this.

Buddhist symbols

The lotus flower

The **lotus flower** is an important symbol for **Buddhism**, meaning 'transformation'. It is a symbol of purity and growth. The lotus flower appears on the surface of a lake and is beautiful to see. Its roots are buried deep within the mud of the lake. The **Buddha** saw this as a symbol for human life – we might be stuck in the mud of human existence, but we can still come to an **enlightenment**, even in the midst of all the murk!

One of the important Buddhist scriptures is called the **Lotus Sutra**.

In meditation, some Buddhists sit in the lotus position in order to help them gain peace.

Read the signs

Symbols can have a number of uses. They can warn us about something, such as a dangerous road ahead. They can give us instructions and they can give us information. In the religious world, signs and symbols can act in these ways, as well many others.

The wheel of life

The **wheel of life** is another important symbol. The eight spokes in the wheel stand for the **Eightfold Path** that the Buddha advised people to follow. It reminds Buddhists that they are all trapped on the cycle of birth-death-birth-death-birth which they can only escape from when they stop being attached to being 'someone living somewhere'. By letting go into the state of **nirvana**, Buddhists experience a boundless state of freedom and oneness with the universe.

Meditating in the lotus position helps Buddhists to gain peace·

In the centre of the wheel of life are the cockerel, the snake and the pig. They stand for the three poisons that can corrupt the mind – greed, hatred and ignorance (or delusion).

Over the top of the wheel is Yama, a demon, who reminds us that this is a world of change and decay.

The six realms inside the wheel show various parts of the journey a person might make in order to become enlightened. In each of these, there is a Buddha, showing that enlightenment is possible at any stage and in any place, if a person truly wishes to find it. The six realms are states of mind that can be experienced every day to find release from the Buddha's wisdom.

Buddha rupas

There are many different images of the Buddha, which are called **rupas**.

A sitting Buddha shows the importance of meditation. The Buddha in the lotus position shows him teaching the **Dharma**.

Making a mandala

There are other images that remind Buddhists of their religion. For example, a riderless horse reminds them of the sacrifice that the Buddha made when he left the palace in order to join the holy men.

Another way of showing beauty in a world of constant change and decay is by making **mandalas**, special patterns made from coloured sand, because these can never remain permanent.

A sitting Buddha rupa

Learning about religion

❶ Write a story about someone to show the idea of the lotus as a symbol of truth for Buddhists.

❷ Design your own wheel of life which shows the Buddha's teaching.

❸ Which of the images of the Buddha do you like most? Explain why this is the case.

Learning from religion

❶ Create a symbol for wisdom.

❷ 'Making mandalas is truly pointless.' What do you think?

The Bodhisattvas

In this section you will:

● learn about the importance to **Mahayana Buddhists** of the idea of the **Bodhisattvas**, the enlightened beings who try to help people find **enlightenment**

● reflect on the importance of role models in your personal development.

Avalokitesvara

Heroes or zeros

Many of us love stories about heroes and superheroes such as Superman or Batman. Perhaps we admire their bravery.

Or perhaps we admire a famous sports personality or pop star. We might try to read everything they say. We might try to live our lives in the way they live theirs. Sometimes they can be role models of how to live a good life or they can be people who show us how not to live a bad life. Choosing a good role-model is something we all need to do.

Enlightened beings

In Mahayana Buddhism, there are a group of beings called Bodhisattvas. They are '**Buddhas** to be', beings who have attained enlightenment but choose to stay back from **nirvana** so that they can lead others to enlightenment. Sometimes, these beings may return as human beings (Tibetan Buddhists think that the **Dalai Lama** is a Bodhisattva).

Bodhisattvas are also often symbols for a characteristic that the Buddha had or that the individual Buddhist should try to obtain. The most important of these characteristics are wisdom and compassion.

Avalokitesvara

This Bodhisattva stands for perfect compassion. He is keen to help Buddhists to find solutions to the problems they face in their daily lives as well as to help them reach the goals of enlightenment and nirvana.

Tara

Tara is a Bodhisattva who is said to have sprouted from the side of **Avalokitesvara** and who helps in the process of enlightenment.

Tara

Maitreya

Maitreya

For many Buddhists, **Maitreya** is the most important of the Bodhisattvas. They believe that he will one day come to earth and bring in a golden age of wisdom and peace. His teachings will be so powerful and his leadership so wise that he will be known as a second Buddha. Although he currently lives in a heavenly realm, he appears to people who experience a heavenly state in order to reveal truths and lead them to enlightenment.

Learning about religion

❶ Why are Bodhisattvas so important to many Buddhists? What problems might reflecting on a Bodhisattva bring to a Buddhist?

❷ Design your own image of a Bodhisattva and explain what quality he/she stands for. Why have you chosen this quality as being so important?

❸ 'Bodhisattvas are really gods by another name.' What might a Buddhist say to this? What do you think? Give reasons for your answers, showing that you have thought about things from more than one point of view.

Learning from religion

❶ Why are role models important to people?

❷ Write about one of the people you regard as a role model and say why they are important to you.

❸ Organize a debate, 'Compassion is more important than wisdom'.

Buddhist devotion

In this section you will:

● find out about some important aspects of Buddhist devotion, or paying respect

● reflect on the things that matter to you most.

What's it worth?

To be a fan is to take something very seriously. If you follow a football team you may well want to own the right shirt, have all the other kit and have a poster. You may want to go to the games or at least watch them on television.

If you are into music, you will want posters, CDs, and to see the artist you like in concert.

People who are fans believe that they need to show the worth of what they think is important by doing things to show their devotion.

Showing respect to the Buddha

Paying respect at home

Buddhists will often visit a **vihara** (temple) or monastery to help them in their spiritual life.

Many Buddhists will also have a shrine in their home. This will contain an image of the **Buddha**, called a **rupa**, as well as flowers, candles, incense and pictures of **Bodhisattvas**.

They will recite the **Three Refuges** and the **Five Moral Precepts** at the shrine. They may well meditate in front of it to help them to focus. They will often burn incense to show their devotion to the Buddha.

Prayer

Many Buddhists do not think of their devotion as prayer. The Buddha is not a god and Buddhism does not teach a belief in a personal god.

When Buddhists pray, they feel that it 'releases the Buddha within'. This means devotion releases the true nature that is trapped inside a person. Some Buddhists see this as a kind of meditation, others talk about it as showing respect to the Buddha.

A Buddhist called Dr Fernado once said:

'Prayer doesn't exist in Buddhism because there is no one to talk to. In my devotions, I say to myself "To the best of my ability, I shall try to emulate the life of the Buddha".'

Flags and wheels

In some Buddhist countries, flags are raised with the words of an important **mantra** written on them. When the wind blows the flag, they believe the blessing of the mantra is released and the energy contained in the thought is carried in the wind.

Tibetan prayer wheels

Similarly, some Buddhists use prayer wheels to release the prayers into the environment.

Beads and bells

Many Buddhists will use **mala beads** to help them meditate. There are 108 mala beads on a string, which help them to focus on an object and to release interfering thoughts.

Some Buddhists will use bells to help them. In Tibet, a bell is seen as a symbol of wisdom.

Some Buddhists may hold a **varja** in their hands whilst meditating. This is a symbol of the Buddha's power and truth behind all things.

Learning about religion

❶ Design a display to show how important artefacts are to Buddhists.

❷ Which items used in Buddhist devotion most surprise you? Explain your selection.

❸ 'The Buddha would have discouraged prayer.' How might a Buddhist respond to this statement?

Learning from religion

❶ What is the most important thing in your life? Explain why.

❷ 'Prayer is a waste of time.' Organize a class debate about this and/or write a speech on this, showing that you have thought about it from more than one point of view.

Meditation

Think it through

If you get stuck in Maths, you may need to think through a problem for quite a while before you come to a solution that will help you.

If you have an argument with someone, you might be told that you ought to think before you speak!

We often need time to think through things before our actions result in consequences that could be very destructive or negative.

Buddhist meditation

The **Buddha** had his **enlightenment** experience as a result of meditation. For Buddhists today, meditation is a powerful technique to help them work with the mind in order to gain understanding. Meditation enables them to train their mind to make it fit, just as jogging enables a body to get fit. The following are two examples of how a Buddhist might meditate.

Thinking it through

A monk meditating: meditation is an important Buddhist practice

Breathe in slowly through your nose and as you do so, feel relaxed. Use your breath as a focus of your attention so that your mind does not wander off with thoughts. As you breathe out, feel the tensions in your body leaving you. Try to concentrate on the rhythm of your breathing.

Imagine that you are in a large room. See the people who care for you there. Try to look at their faces very carefully. Now see any brother or sisters that you have there. Now see any other relatives you have – aunties, uncles, cousins, grandparents. Try to see all your family around you.
Now try to see in your mind those people you think are your friends. Picture them in your mind clearly. See friends, family, relatives all standing around you in a large room. Now try to picture in your mind the face of someone you do not like and, instead of feeling hatred or anger, generate warmth to them.

Meditation has many aims. Meditation can help Buddhists realize the meaning of the great truths of the Buddha and enable them to gain awareness of things in their own lives that need changing and developing. Because it leads to clarity, understanding and calm, meditation also leads to freedom from suffering. It is helpful to use some characteristics that the Buddha thought were supportive. These were called the **Brahma Viharas**, or 'spiritual friends', and include the following:

1. **metta**, or loving kindness – being gentle and tender to all

2. **karuna**, or compassion – an understanding and concern for others

3. **mudita**, or sympathetic joy – showing delight in the success of others

4. **upekkah**, or evenness of mind – showing a balanced approach to life.

Meditation can be practised both alone and in groups at the local Buddhist centre or temple.

Learning about religion

1. Draw a spider diagram to show all the reasons a Buddhist might practice meditation.

2. 'Meditation is a waste of time.' How would a Buddhist reply to this?

3. 'The Brahma Viharas are impossible to develop.' How might a Buddhist answer this?

Learning from religion

1. Write down the feelings and responses you had to the two meditations. Why do you think you reacted in these ways?

2. How could you develop ways to show the Brahma Viharas in your life?

Buddhist holy places

Important places

Try to think about the places you have been to during your life. Perhaps you remember a holiday in a really beautiful place which you really enjoyed. Or perhaps it was a visit to a theme park which you enjoyed most.

The vihara

Buddhists, like other religious people, often have important places where they go to pay respect. One name for such a place is the **vihara**.

A Buddhist vihara

The vihara is sometimes attached to a monastery but not always. The vihara contains a shrine room where Buddhists meet to meditate, pray and celebrate important festivals.

In the shrine room, there are several important items. Often, the room is dominated by a statue of the **Buddha**, which is used as a focus of intention and a reminder of his teaching. There may be other pictures of the Buddha and other important Buddhist figures in the room as well.

Often by the statue you will find flowers, incense sticks and candles. The flowers are a symbol to remind the assembly that the Buddha taught that life is always changing. The incense sticks represent **Dharma** (truth) and are offered to show the intention to live a life of good deeds and truthfulness. The candle is a symbol of the wisdom and insight that can be found in the Buddha and the Dharma.

Other types of building

There are many other types of holy buildings in the Buddhist faith.

A stupa in Thailand

A wat in Wimbledon

A pagoda in Battersea

People often call Buddhist places of worship temples but they have many other names too. In Thailand, Buddhists worship in a building called a **wat**.

A **stupa** is very special. Each stupa is shaped like a bell, because bells are used to call Buddhists to meditation. These buildings contain a relic from the Buddha or from an important Buddhist leader.

The temple in Kandy in Sri Lanka is said to contain Buddha's tooth (see page 36), and is a place of pilgrimage.

A **pagoda** is another type of building which is important to Buddhists. It is built in five sections. These remind Buddhists that the universe has five basic elements – earth, fire, water, wind and space. Sometimes these buildings are also called **dagodas**.

Shrines at home

Not all **meditation** happens in the temples or the viharas. Buddhists often set aside a space or even an entire room in their homes as places to pay respect and to meditate.

Learning about religion

❶ Draw and label a diagram of a shrine room.

❷ 'You don't need holy buildings to be a Buddhist.' How would a Buddhist reply to this? What do you think? Show that you have thought about it from more than one point of view.

❸ Write a poem about the five elements Buddhists believe make up the world.

Learning from religion

❶ What place matters to you most and why?

❷ The Buddhist holy places can be full of noise or very silent. Which do you prefer to be and why?

❸ Organize a debate, 'Truly religious people would not waste money on buildings when there are poor in the world to be fed.'

Buddhist scriptures

Preserving the past

There are many ways in which we know about the past. Archaeologists may dig up artefacts such as pots, coins and weapons from long ago. There are castles and other buildings which are still used today, but also tell us things about the past.

Yet one of the most important ways we can learn about the past is through the books that people in the past wrote.

The Three Baskets

The **Buddha's** teaching was passed down the years and preserved in the chants of the **Sangha**.

The Buddha's followers did not originally think that it was important to write down the stories of the Buddha. Most scholars think that the first Buddhist holy books were written down about 500 years after the time of the Buddha.

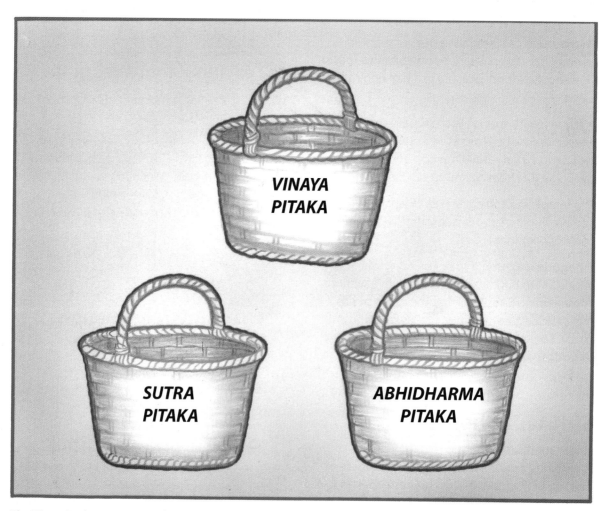

The Three Baskets

In the gap between the books being written and the time of the Buddha, the stories and teachings were passed down by word of mouth. People had to train their memories to remember important ideas because there were not as many opportunities to write or to store information and the teachings of the Buddha.

In 30 BCE, a group of monks gathered on the island of Sri Lanka. They gathered together a book which is known as the **Tripitaka**, or the Three Baskets.

The Three Baskets are:

1. the **Vinaya Pitaka** – these are the rules that only monks and nuns have to follow and stories about how they were formed

2. the **Sutra Pitaka** – this is a collection of teachings given by the Buddha

3. the **Abhidharma Pitaka** – these are teachings about the way in which we look at the world around us.

Other scriptures

According to Buddhist teachings, the Buddha had lived many other lifetimes as animals and other humans. There are a number of stories about these other lives, which have been collected together to form the **Jataka** tales. There are 540 Jataka tales in total.

The **Dharmapada** is another important scripture, because it brings together some of the Buddha's sayings (423 verses in total). Here are a selection:

'One should give up anger – one should abandon pride.'

Verse 221

'Self-conquest is indeed far better than the conquest of others.'

Verse 104

'Better than a thousand useless words is one single word that brings peace.'

Verse 100

In India, in the first century CE, they began to collect teachings from the time of the Buddha. The Chinese began to collect their material a century later.

There are other important books in Buddhism which are developments of the Buddha's teachings. One example is the Tibetan *Book of the Dead*. This was written to help people prepare for their next life and to think about the consequences of the way they have lived.

Learning about religion

1. Draw a labelled diagram to show the Three Baskets and what they contain.

2. Does it matter that the holy books of Buddhism were written down 500 years after the time of the Buddha? Show that you have thought about this from more than one point of view.

3. The Jataka stories use the other lifetimes of the Buddha in order to make or reinforce some point from his teaching. Do you think this is a good way to teach people difficult ideas? Give reason for your answers.

Learning from religion

1. 'Buddhist holy books are irrelevant to the world today.' What would a Buddhist say to this? What do you think?

2. Look at one of the sayings in the section from the Dharmapada and devise a play to show the meaning of the saying.

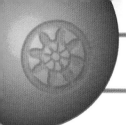

The festival of Wesak

In this section you will:

- learn about the Buddhist festival of **Wesak** and its importance to Buddhist people
- reflect on the importance of celebrations in people's lives.

Celebrations

It is very important that we have times to celebrate, times when we can have parties to mark important events. It may be New Year or our birthday, or when we see our team win an event.

We all need to enjoy the good things in life, to say that life is worth living and to show what we think is most important.

Wesak

Wesak (called '**Buddha** Day' by some Buddhists) is the most important festival of the Buddhist year. It celebrates the most important events in the life of the Buddha – his birth, his **enlightenment** and when he died and entered in the state of **parinirvana**. Buddhists believe that all of these three things happened on the same day in different years. The celebration takes place at the time of the full moon in late May or June.

Washing the images of the Buddha

Wesak in Thailand

In Thailand, Wesak is a very important day. Many Buddhists will visit a monastery, taking with them flowers, a candle and a stick of incense. The candle's lighted wick is a sign of wisdom, whilst the melted wax and the flowers are a sign that nothing is permanent. The incense represents truth and is a sign of devotion to the Buddha.

People also will walk around a **stupa** three times, in order to show their commitment to following the Buddha, the **Dharma** and the **Sangha** in their lives. Some will water bodhi trees, to remind them that it was under such a tree that the Buddha came to understand the truth.

Houses are cleaned and statues of the Buddha are washed. Fish that have been caught days earlier are released back into the river to show how the Buddha's teaching brings freedom. Birds are often released from cages as another image of the freedom that they are celebrating.

Wesak in Sri Lanka

In Sri Lanka, huge paintings of events from the life of the Buddha are put on display. Lanterns are hung. Street performers such as acrobats and dancers perform.

It is a time to share the best things in life with other people, so often wayside stalls of food and drink are set up to help people who may have travelled long distances to come to the festival ceremonies.

During the festival, Buddhists may decide to follow five more moral precepts. These are normally kept just by monks and nuns. They are:

- not eating after midday
- not sleeping on a comfortable bed
- not watching any form of entertainment, for example, going to the theatre
- not wearing jewellery or any scent
- not handling any money.

In some Mahayana countries, the birth of the Buddha is celebrated at the Festival of Hana Matsuri. Statues of the Buddha are decorated with spring flowers.

Learning about religion

❶ Why do you think that Wesak is so important to Buddhists?

❷ Choose three symbols or three actions performed at the festival of Wesak and draw a diagram with captions illustrating them.

❸ 'The Buddha would have disapproved of Wesak.' What do you think? Show that you have thought about this from more than one point of view.

Learning from religion

❶ 'Human beings need celebrations.' Draw a spider diagram to show as many reasons as you can to say why people need celebrations.

❷ 'All these festivals prove that Buddhism is a religion like the others.' Look at the information on Wesak and the other festivals and say what you think, showing that you have thought about it from more than one point of view.

Other Buddhist festivals

New Year

New Year is often an important celebration for both religious and non-religious people. It enables them to reflect on what has happened in the past year, to take stock. It is also a time to think about the future. Some people make resolutions to change or improve themselves in the year ahead.

Songkran

In Thailand, New Year doesn't happen on 1 January, but takes place in the middle of April.

The festival of **Songkran** is a time to celebrate the new year.

Songkran is a festival that relies on water. Thai people splash each other with water as part of the celebration of a new start.

There are colourful parades, boat races, masks and dances. A princess of the festival is elected.

When the festival ends, Thai people will put on new sets of clothes.

They will also release fish they have previously caught into rivers, a sign of the release that **enlightenment** brought to the **Buddha**.

Festival of the Tooth

The Festival of the Tooth takes place on the island of Sri Lanka. Buddhists believe that one of the Buddha's teeth has been kept in a specially built building called a **stupa**.

The tooth is kept inside caskets and these are not brought out until the festival takes place.

Songkran can get you very wet!

Elephants at the Festival of the Tooth

On the night of the full moon in August, there is a procession of elephants, led by one that is decked out in golden materials.

The procession includes dancers, jugglers and other street entertainers, as well as the monks who care for the casket.

Obon

Obon is a festival celebrated by Japanese Buddhists. It happens on 13 July. It reminds Buddhists of a time when the Buddha rescued the mother of one of his disciples from a hell.

It is a time to pay respects to the ancestors, so Buddhists will clean the graves of their departed relatives with water and also adorn them with flowers.

Prayers are offered for the dead relatives and then incense is burnt in order to encourage their spirits to return to the world from which they came.

At the end of the festival, a huge bonfire is lit at Mount Daimonjiyama outside the city of Kyoto.

Learning about religion

❶ Design a diagram to explain what happens during the festival of Songkran.

❷ Do you think the Buddha would be pleased with the Festival of the Tooth, which celebrates a part of his body? Give reasons for your answer, showing you have thought about it from more than one point of view.

❸ Why do you think ancestors are so important to Japanese Buddhists?

Learning from religion

❶ Why do you think people make New Year's resolutions?

❷ Do you think it is a good idea to have a special time to celebrate the dead? Give reasons for your answers.

Obon is a time to remember those who have died

Buddhist pilgrimage

In this section you will:
- find out about some of the important places of pilgrimage for Buddhists
- reflect on the importance of special places to people.

We all need a place to get away to…

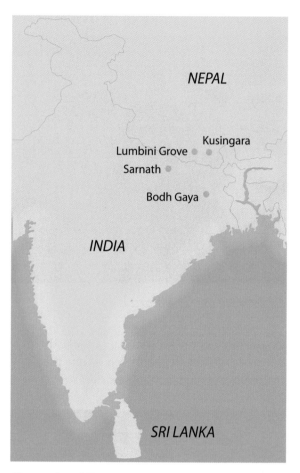

Places of Buddhist pilgrimage

Special places

We all need to get away from the stresses of normal life. When we go on holiday, we go to places where we believe we will find rest and relaxation.

Lumbini Grove

'The place, **Ananda**, at which the devoted person can say, "Here the **Buddha** was born" is a spot to be visited with feelings of reverence.'

The **Buddha** was born in **Lumbini Grove** in Nepal. When he was born, Buddhists believe that the earth was filled with light and shook in expectation. He was brought up in the area.

The great Buddhist King Asoka built a pillar to point out that it was here the Buddha was born.

Bodh Gaya

'The place, Ananda, at which the devoted person can say, "Here the Buddha attained supreme and highest wisdom" is a spot to be visited with feelings of reverence.'

At **Bodh Gaya**, sitting beneath a bodhi tree, **Siddhartha Gautama** received the **enlightenment** that led him to become the Buddha.

A bodhi tree grows today in the spot where Buddhists believe the first one was located. The tree is adorned with prayer flags.

Pilgrims come to the tree to worship and to meditate. There are many temples in the area.

A shrine near the bodhi tree at Bodh Gaya

Sarnath

'The place, Ananda, at which the devoted person can say, "Here the wheel of the **Dharma** was set in motion by the Buddha" is a spot to be visited with feelings of reverence.'

It was at the Deer Park in **Sarnath** that the Buddha preached his first sermon, in which he explained his teachings on the meaning of and solution to suffering. The holy men, who had once abandoned him, became his first disciples.

Kusingara

'The place, Ananda, at which the devoted person can say, "Here the Buddha passed finally away" is a spot to be visited with feelings of reverence.'

It was at the house of **Chunda** that the Buddha ate the meal that contained the food that would lead to his death. For Buddhists, this is a place of great holiness as it was here that the Buddha completed his personal journey to **nirvana**.

Learning about religion

❶ Why are pilgrimages important to Buddhist people? Give three reasons.

❷ Which is the most important of the four places to visit? Give reasons for your answer.

❸ 'You cannot really understand Buddhism until you've been to the places where it started.' What do you think about this statement? What do you think a Buddhist might say?

Learning from religion

❶ 'All life is a pilgrimage.' What does this mean? How far do you think this statement is true?

❷ Write about a place that is very special to you. Why it is so special?

❸ Design a poster to explain the importance of pilgrimage in Buddhism and one other religion.

Living in a monastery

In this section you will:
- find about the importance of the monastic life in Buddhism
- reflect on the importance of self-discipline.

Joining a monastery

There are Buddhist monasteries all across the world, including in the United Kingdom.

In some Buddhist countries such as Thailand, a young boy may well become a monk for a short time in his childhood as a way of getting good **karma** for himself and his family. It is also a very good way of getting a good education, because the monasteries are the main places to learn in many Asian countries.

If he decides to stay in the monastery, the boy will go to a special school in the monastery. If he stays long enough to want to become a full adult member of the community, he will go through two stages:

1 as a **samanera** – at this stage, he is what is known as a novice and is on probation to see if it is a good idea for him to stay

A boy's head is shaved as he joins a monastery

2 as a **bhikkhu** – he has to be at least 20 before he can reach this stage. To become a bhikku is to make the formal promise to stay a monk for the rest of your life.

There are many tests that a person has to go through before they will be fully accepted into the life of the monastery.

What effect does joining the monastery have?

Having decided to become an ordained monk, the candidate will have his head and beard shaved. To remove hair is a sign that the monk is prepared to put aside vanity and to realize that all things are subject to change and that nothing is permanent.

When he has received his robe from the community, he will be given an alms bowl. In Thailand he may be given sandals, needle and thread, a string of beads, a razor, an umbrella and a net to drain out insects from his drinking water. In UK monasteries, a monk owns his own robe and his bowl, though he may be given the use of other items.

At the ceremony, five monks have to mark out the boundaries of the monastery. Then the candidate will kneel in front of the senior monk, normally called the abbot.

The candidate asks the abbot for permission to become a member. The abbot recites a meditation about how all human life is perishable. The candidate asks for forgiveness, promises that he will not boast, that he is committed to the **Buddha**, **Dharma** and the **Sangha** and that he will follow the rules of the monastery.

The candidate has to state that his parents have accepted his calling, that he is a free man, free from debt and employment, and that he is

The things a monk can own

human and male! He will be given a Buddhist name by the abbot, normally one that suggests a quality that he could develop.

In the UK, both monks and nuns can be ordained.

Chithurst Monastery in Sussex

Life in a monastery

Monks may live in forest dwellings or help to run the local **vihara**. If their monastery is large, they may well run a school.

In England, some monasteries are located in large houses in the countryside, like the one pictured, at Chithurst in Sussex.

Both in the UK and in other countries, there are also shared and separate monasteries for nuns. They have to follow many of the same rules as the monks, including shaving their heads.

Learning about religion

❶ Write a diary from the point of view of a boy in a monastery.

❷ What do you think would attract a person to becoming a monk?

❸ Devise a radio advert to attract people to become Buddhist monks and nuns (use information from this section and the next).

Learning from religion

❶ If you could own ten things, what would they be and why?

❷ 'Being a monk is the act of someone running away from the world, not someone really trying to help it.' Reading this section and the next, how do you think a Buddhist monk might answer this? What do you think?

❸ What are the pluses and minuses of living life as a monk?

Being in a community

In this section you will:

● learn more about what it means to belong to a monastery and why these are still important to Buddhist people today

● reflect on whether you could radically change your lifestyle.

Following the rules

Many people find following rules very difficult indeed. Some people even say that rules are made to be broken.

Try playing a board game or a football match without rules, and it just won't work. If a person were to ignore rules when they were driving a car, someone would soon get hurt.

We might not like rules but we might find that we often need them to keep us safe or to help us enjoy the best of life.

The intentions of a monastery

Buddhists have to follow the **Five Moral Precepts**, but monks and nuns are expected to follow not only these, but others as well. These include:

1 not to overeat

2 not to sing, dance or be entertained

3 not to wear jewellery or perfume, or beautify themselves

4 not to sleep in a high or broad bed

5 not to handle money.

Some of the things a monk has to give up

The **Vinaya**, or rules, are followed because **Buddhism** is a personal training system based on restraint and giving up things rather than a system to keep monks or nuns in line. The reason for the training is to be free from desire. The more simple the lifestyle without luxury – with only food, shelter and medicine – the less chance for feelings of desire.

By wearing jewellery, perfume or flowers, the monks and nuns would be attracting attention to themselves. By sleeping on a simple bed, they prove that they are not idle.

All monks are given alms bowls, but they are not allowed to receive money directly. The alms bowls will normally be the place where Buddhists will put gifts of food. They can also offer practical support for the work of the local monastery.

Each monastery may well have its own set of rules, according to its own tradition, for example, the **Theravadan** Vinaya try to follow 227 rules. The Zen or Tibetan Vinaya may differ from this.

The Chithurst monastery in Sussex stresses the value of the following precepts amongst lay Buddhists and the monastic community, which extends these to 227 precepts. The Five Moral Precepts are:

1 *to avoid taking life* – not to hurt a living thing, be it human or animal

2 *to avoid taking what is not given* – stealing is strictly forbidden

3 *to avoid sexual misconduct* – celibacy for monks means that they are not to take part in any sexual behaviour

4 *to avoid speaking falsely* – not to speak in a way that is offensive or proud

5 *to avoid drink and drugs that can cloud the mind* – to refrain from taking drugs and alcohol which could hinder clear-mindedness.

Daily life in the monastery

At the Chithurst monastery, the day begins at 5.00am with chanting and **meditation** sessions. There is time for breakfast and performing some morning duties before the next meditation at 7.30am. There is a meeting to decide on the morning and afternoon jobs to be done before they sit down for the main and only meal of the day. This is served at 10.30am and is followed by a rest time, then time to perform more tasks. In the afternoon, there is a cup of tea and then the monks retire at 9.00pm. On some evenings, chanting and meditation last through the night.

Learning about religion

1 Why do you think the monasteries have the rules they have?

2 Organize a class discussion about which rules you think should be changed in order to make monastery life more relevant.

3 How do you think monks help the Buddhist community? See if you can find out more details by using the Internet to connect you to Buddhist websites.

Learning from religion

1 'Spending all day meditating is a waste of time.' What might a Buddhist monk say in response to this? What do you think? Give reasons or your answer.

2 'Living with other people helps you to become a better person.' How true do you think this is?

3 'Rules aren't really necessary when people are trying not to be selfish.' How true do you think this?

Birth

In this section you will:

● find out about the way some Buddhists celebrate the birth of children and the ideas attached to these ceremonies

● reflect on the importance of birth.

Birthdays

Birthdays can be very important to all of us. Most of us love to receive presents and cards, to know that other people have given us signs that they love and care for us.

Birth ceremonies in Buddhism

Buddhists often mark the birth of a child with what is called a birth blessing. Here, the child is given a blessing on entering the world but their Buddhist name as a lay person or an adult will be given later.

In some countries, such as Myanmar (Burma), the family will gather at the birth of a child to celebrate. They will give the child a cradle and will put gifts in it.

The gifts are normally those considered to be helpful for the child. If they are male, they are normally things such as books and tools, for example hammers. If they are female, they may well be given a needle and some thread.

Birthdays can be important celebrations

A child is very precious to its parents

In **Theravada** countries, monks may well sprinkle the child with water, as a sign that they wish the child to be blessed in the future. A wax candle may well be dripped into some water, as a sign that the child belongs to the four elements of earth, air, fire and water.

Importance of family life for the Buddha

The **Buddha** believed that family life was very important to help us grow as people.

He once compared the family to a group of trees in the forest. They are able to support each other and give each other protection against the wind. We need our families to help us, he said.

When a child is about a month old, in some Buddhist countries, his or her hair might be shaved off, because some Buddhists believe that hair links the child back to the bad **karma** of its previous life. It is a way of saying that a new life is a new start and that the problems of the past should be forgotten to make a better future possible. Other Buddhists think that this is just a superstition which has been justified by bringing Buddhist ideas into its practice.

Monks are invited to the ceremony. They may be asked to give the child a name that reflects the qualities that the child might aspire to, or name them after a great Buddhist from the past. Monks will normally chant scriptures on behalf of the child.

In Thailand, the parents will often give the monks food as a gift in order to win good karma for the child. In other countries, food is given to the monks to recognize that their teaching nourishes the spiritual life.

In some Buddhist countries, a sacred thread may be wound around the wrist of the child as a sign that they wish the child to receive blessing.

Learning about religion

❶ Why do you think that birth ceremonies are so important to Buddhist people? Give reasons.

❷ 'Buddhist birth ceremonies can be sexist.' How might a Buddhist answer this? Give reasons for your answer.

❸ Design a leaflet for a Buddhist temple to give out to explain about Buddhist birth ceremonies. Use information from Buddhist Internet sites.

Learning from religion

❶ Do you think everyone – both religious and non-religious – should have a formal naming ceremony? Explain your views.

❷ 'Buddhism isn't really interested in birth.' What would a Buddhist say? What do you think?

❸ Assemble your own birth ceremony and write/act it out.

Marriage

Committed for life?

Marriage, for many people, is a way of publicly saying before your family, friends, the community and, for some, before God, that you intend to stay together in a loving relationship. Of course, it doesn't always work out like that.

Many people decide to live with someone without having a marriage ceremony. They feel they can be committed to each other without visiting a religious building or a registry office.

Marriage in Buddhist countries

Buddhist countries all differ in their marriage customs, but there are some things that are common to all of them.

In some, but not all, Buddhist countries, the choice of husband or wife is through an arranged marriage, when two sets of parents come together in order to set up a marriage. In many Buddhist countries, marriage is a result of the couple's choice, not their parents'.

In a country like Thailand, the wedding will take place in the bride's home, where monks will be invited to bless the couple and to recite scriptures to encourage them.

Monks do not actually perform the marriage, but a relative, such as the uncle of the bride, will do. In the UK, Buddhist marriages are blessed rather than performed at a monastery.

A Buddhist wedding

A monk can bless the newly married couple

The couple will stand on a special platform called a **purowa**, which is decorated with white flowers.

During the ceremony, they will exchange rings, and vows will be made by each partner. A silk scarf will be wrapped around their hands as a way of saying that they have been joined together as husband and wife.

In **Theravada** Buddhist countries, a thread of cotton is passed around the temple where the marriage is to take place. Two pieces of the thread will then be cut. A monk will wrap one around the wrist of the bridegroom and then the bridegroom will be handed the other thread. He will then wind this around the wrist of his bride, because monks are not allowed to touch a woman as part of their monastic vows.

It is the tradition that after the wedding ceremonies, there is a large feast bought by the family and friends.

In order for the new relationship to get off to a good start, the couple or their parents will make a gift of food to the monks as a way of gaining good **karma** and also to support the monks.

Learning about religion

❶ Find out more about Buddhist weddings by using the Internet. Use the information to write a short talk about Buddhist weddings.

❷ What are the most important symbols in a Buddhist marriage? Write about what they mean.

❸ 'The Buddha showed no commitment to marriage in the way he left his wife when he sought the holy life.' What would a Buddhist say to this? What would you say?

Learning from religion

❶ Write down in two columns what you think are the advantages and the disadvantages of arranged marriages.

❷ What qualities do you think you need to be a good bridesmaid and/or a best man at a wedding?

❸ 'Marriage is out of date.' Organize a class debate about this.

Death

In this section you will:

● learn about the Buddhist beliefs surrounding death and how they mark the passing of someone

● reflect on how to deal with questions of grief and bereavement.

The ultimate statistic

The playwright George Bernard Shaw said that death was the ultimate statistic because 'one in one die'.

But how do we mark someone's passing, and how do we deal with our grief at their going?

A Buddhist cemetery

A Buddhist funeral procession in Myanmar (Burma)

Buddhist funerals

Buddhist funerals are different in different countries.

In Sri Lanka, funeral ceremonies are not times of mourning but can become an opportunity to improve the **karma** of the dead person as they move to their next life.

The body is prepared by washing it and then the hands are clasped together. Three times a thread is wound round the deceased's hands, as a sign of three things that have tied them to this world – money, marriage and children.

Several other items are placed in the coffin:

1. a small ladder, which will enable the mind of the deceased to leave the body behind

2. flowers and incense – these are signs that life is impermanent and leads only surely to death

3. a small set of flags, which will assist a person's arrival in the heavens.

The funeral will normally take place in a local monastery. The body will be cremated on a pyre.

A monk will later gather the ashes of the deceased and recite a scripture reminding the relatives how short life is.

Some of the bones of the deceased may be turned in a half circle to show the reality of life, and then turned to the east to show death. The pieces of bone and ash are then collected and buried in an urn. If the person who has died was felt to be especially holy, he or she may have a relic preserved in a **stupa**.

Funerals in Mahayana countries

In countries such as China, Taiwan and Korea, special attention is given to honouring the dead ancestors. When a person dies, a monk will place a tablet in their memory on the family shrine in their home.

The monk will apply 'last water' to the deceased and wash the body.

Friends and neighbours often celebrate with a vegetarian meal. They will also burn incense at the graveyard.

Families will continue to formally mourn after the death of their relative as a way of securing good merit for the person who has died.

Relatives may also give gifts to the monks for their support during this time.

One Buddhist writer has written:

No weeping, nor yet sorrowing,
Nor any kind of mourning aids,
Departed one, whose kin remain,
(Unhelped by their action) thus.

From *Minor Readings* by Bhikkhu Naranoni

Learning about religion

1. Write about or design a diagram to explain about the important symbols in a Buddhist funeral in Sri Lanka.

2. How might monks help Buddhists by being a part of the funeral of a loved one? Give reasons for your answer.

3. Why do you think washing the body is so important to Buddhists?

Learning from religion

1. Should you celebrate a life or mourn most at a funeral? Give reasons for your answer, showing that you have thought about it from more than one point of view.

2. 'Buddhism is obsessed with death but has little to teach us about living.' What would a Buddhist say to this? What do you think?

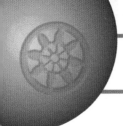

The environment

In this section you will:

● find out about the key ideas that Buddhists have that affect the way they treat the environment

● reflect on the important issues concerning the environment and how we can improve things.

What a wonderful world

We live in a beautiful world, but it has often been ruined or damaged by the actions of human beings. For example, the aerosols we have used in the past have contributed to the greenhouse effect which has led to climate change.

Oil spills from tankers have often ruined large areas of the sea and coastline, leading to the deaths of many birds and other forms of wildlife.

Humans have often made decisions that have made the world a less than beautiful place.

Do no harm

Buddhists believe that they should do no harm to any living thing. This is called **ahimsa**. For many Buddhists, this means that they do all they can to avoid killing any form of life.

Monks, for example, are given a strainer so that they do not swallow insects by mistake when drinking.

Pollution can damage the earth

One Buddhist left a trail of sugar in order to encourage some ants to leave the kitchen rather than using ant powder which would have killed them.

So who made the earth?

Buddhists say they do not believe in a Creator God who made the planet because they do not know this from first-hand experience. But they do not deny a Creator God, either. They believe in creating a better world through wise choices and harmless living.

Karma

As we have seen, Buddhists believe that all actions have consequences. This is known as **karma**. If we choose to live in a way that damages others, we will cause effects for them and the planet.

The environment will also be affected by the whole group of humanity, so people need to encourage governments and other groups who work for the environment. As the Buddhist writer Tich Nhat Hanh put it:

'Non-violent action born of awareness is the most effective way to confront adversity.'

Tich Nhat Hanh, *Love is Action*

'As the Bee takes the essence of a flower and flies around without destroying its beauty and perfume, so let the sage (the wise person) wander in this life.'

Dharmapada 49

Do not take what is not given

One of the **Five Moral Precepts** which the **Buddha** gave to his followers was that they should not take what is not given to them.

Buddhists do not abuse the environment. If they have to take from the environment, then they will put things back into it. For example, if a tree is cut down, a Buddhist would plant a tree to replace it.

Buddhists teach that all of nature is interconnected and that we need to make sure that we care for it, as we are an important part of it.

Learning about religion

❶ What does ahimsa mean to the way Buddhists should behave towards the environment?

❷ Write a leaflet for a Buddhist environmental group. Use the Internet to research more about Buddhist beliefs in this area.

❸ Draw a diagram to show how one person's actions can affect the rest of the world.

Learning from religion

❶ 'Do not take what is non given.' How might this teaching be put into practice by:
   a individuals
   b companies
   c countries?

❷ 'Buddhists are so interested in nirvana that they don't really care about this world.' What would Buddhists say to this? What do you think? Show that you have considered more than one point of view.

❸ What could you do to improve the environment around you?

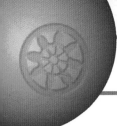

Wealth and poverty

In this section you will:

● find out about Buddhist attitudes to wealth and poverty

● reflect on the issues of wealth and poverty as they affect the world today.

One world?

Economists (people who study how money is made and the consequences of the way it is spent) say that the world could be divided into two groups:

1. the developed nations – these are the richest countries in the world and include the USA, Germany, the UK and Australia

2. the developing nations – these are nations which are said to be developing rather than rich or wealthy.

In the developing nations, thousands of children die every day because of the consequences of hunger. Millions die before their fifth birthday because they contract diseases such as measles.

Buddhist teaching on wealth and poverty

Siddhartha was born into great wealth, but he chose to live the life of the poor holy men he had encountered on his visits to the city.

He realized that neither poverty nor riches, neither pleasure nor pain was the way to achieve the truth he sought.

The **Buddha** taught that what was necessary was a **Middle Way** between the two extremes. So a Buddhist today would argue that we need a balance – enough food for everyone's needs, but not enough for their greed.

Buddhism teaches care of the poor

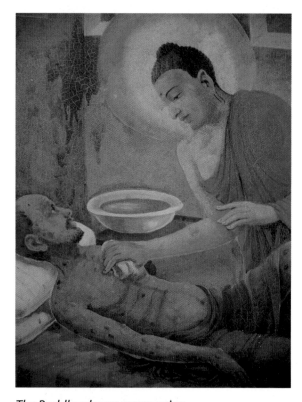

The Buddha shows compassion

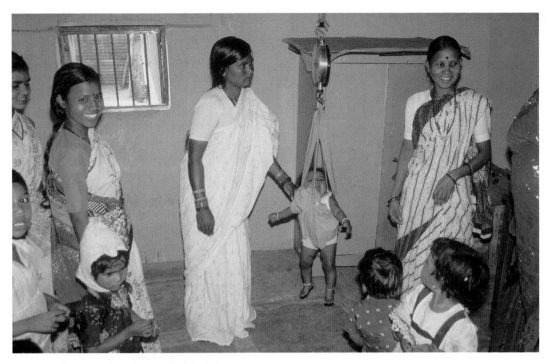

Bringing hope and healing

The Buddha also taught that 'Desire leads to pain.' Those who are the victims of the consumption of the rich nations should be thought about – we are all part of the one world and we need to acknowledge this. Buddhists believe that people will never find happiness through the endless acquisition of money and possessions.

Engaged Buddhism

The Buddhist monk Tich Nhat Hanh from Vietnam encouraged Buddhists to think about the consequences of their actions. **Buddhism** is a way of engaging with life and its ultimate aim is to find peace within. This enables Buddhists to care for themselves and for others. By being aware of their intentions, for example, to help or not to help a person, Buddhists believe that **karma** will result.

Many Buddhists in the UK support the Karuna Trust, an organization that works with the very poorest people in the world, trying to make sure they are fed and cared for. It also tries to help in the long-term development of the country.

Learning from religion

❶ How does the Middle Way influence Buddhist teaching on wealth and poverty?

❷ 'The Buddha *chose* poverty – he didn't really understand what it was like to be poor.' What would a Buddhist say to this?

❸ Using the Internet, find out more about and devise a campaign to highlight the work of the Karuna Trust.

Learning from religion

❶ 'Selfishness is the reason why people are poor.' How true is this saying? What else might lead to poverty?

❷ What could you do to help the poor in the world?

Racism

In this section you will:

● find out about the Buddhist teaching on racism and prejudice

● reflect on appropriate reactions to racism.

All the same?

Many people experience some form of name calling or bullying when they are at school. There is something about human nature that means we sometimes pick on those who seem different to us.

A stereotype is a mental picture of a group of people that says that all the members of the group behave in the same way, for example, 'All schoolchildren are trouble!'

Many people have prejudices, that is they have come to a pre-judgement before they meet a person or a group of people about what they are like.

Some people may have the power to discriminate, that is to stop one person getting something they might be entitled to. For example, an employer might refuse to hire someone who is a woman or from a racial minority group. Although the law bans this sort of behaviour, it still happens in some places.

How a Buddhist sees racism

Buddhism teaches that racism is unskilful for a number of reasons.

The **Buddha** talked of three poisons that could cloud the mind. These include ignorance and arrogance, both of which will influence a person to act in a racist way. In the **Eightfold Path**, he taught the need to follow the way of Right

Stereotyping: forming a mental picture of what people should be like

Buddhism teaches compassion and love

Understanding. To judge someone by the colour of their skin or the birthplace of their parents leads to ignorance and suffering. Buddhists believe that judging people stops them from finding the truth because judging fixes the mind in a position that prevents understanding. The part of the path that encourages Right Awareness also takes Buddhists away from being obsessed with themselves and helps them to think about others.

The part of the path that encourages Right Speech should also take the Buddhist believer away from being obsessed with themselves and should make them think about others. They are not to talk in a proud or dismissive way.

In the **Four Noble Truths**, the Buddha taught that there was no such thing as a self. To be a racist is to say that one self is better than another. This attitude fixes a person and does not allow understanding.

Buddhism urges its followers to develop loving kindness (**metta**) to all other living things.

Learning about religion

❶ Which Buddhist teachings do you think are most helpful to stop racism?

❷ 'No Buddhist should ever be racist.' Give three reasons why this should be so.

❸ Devise an advert for a TV or radio station in a Buddhist country to stop racism.

Learning from religion

❶ What makes people racist? Try to list as many ideas as you can.

❷ What could you do to stop racism?

❸ Does religion stop or encourage racism?

Key figures 1

In this section you will:

- learn about the life and teaching of the **Dalai Lama** and come to understand why he is a very important figure for Buddhists today

- reflect on how and if non-violence is appropriate to deal with force.

A special boy

In Tibet, the Buddhist community has been led by a leader with the title Dalai Lama. The Dalai Lama is believed to be the reincarnation of a very sacred **Bodhisattva**, an enlightened being who chooses to continue to be reborn in order to help others to reach the truth.

In 1940, a young boy called Tenzin Gyasto was declared to be the new Dalai Lama. He combined the role of religious leader with being the head of the country. When he was first appointed, he was so young that he had to have others to help him rule.

The Chinese invasion

In 1950, the Chinese invaded Tibet and declared that it would now become a province or part of China. The Chinese gradually took control of the country. In the capital city of Lhasa, many Tibetans rebelled against the Chinese, which led to a crackdown and the execution of many rebels.

The Dalai Lama decided to flee across the border to India, because he believed that he could best help the cause of the Tibetan people by arguing their case from a free country. He realized that he would face either house arrest or execution if he stayed in his country.

The Chinese increasingly attacked the monasteries in Tibet. They destroyed holy books and would take no dissent. They believed that they were freeing the Tibetans from years of pointless, evil traditions. When the Chinese leader, Chairman Mao, died in 1976, much of Lhasa was destroyed.

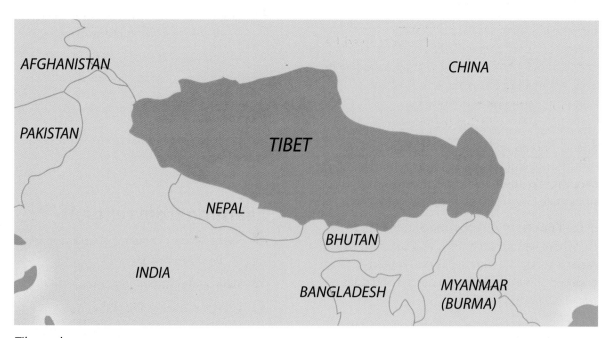

Tibet today

He has written:

'Today we are so interdependent, so closely interconnected that without a sense of universal responsibility, a feeling of universal brotherhood and sisterhood and an understanding and belief that we are all part of one human family, we cannot hope to overcome the damage to our existence – let alone bring peace and happiness.'

One person who has been greatly influenced by the Dalai Lama is the film actor Richard Gere. He established the Gere Foundation and has organized public events to highlight Tibet's problems.

The Dalai Lama

A man of peace

The Dalai Lama is a man committed to peace and, although his country has been occupied, he refuses to advocate a violent response to what has happened.

He has also been prepared to listen to the Chinese and has said that their political beliefs and those of **Buddhism** do not have to be at war with each other.

His work has taken him across the world, speaking on behalf of the Tibetan people and calling for there to be peace in the world.

Learning about religion

❶ Why is the Dalai Lama so special to Tibetan Buddhists?

❷ Write a diary as if you were the Dalai Lama fleeing to India. Tell about your emotions as you leave your country.

❸ Design a wall display to show the history and traditions of Tibet.

Learning from religion

❶ Should the Tibetans have used violence against the Chinese to get their freedom back?

❷ Should you mix religion and politics?

❸ The Dalai Lama was awarded the Nobel Prize for Peace. Find out about other people who have won the Nobel Prize for Peace and have been religious.

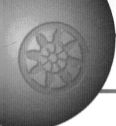

Key figures 2

A monk's tale

Ajahn Sumedho is the leader of a group of Buddhist monks in the **Theravadan** tradition, with monasteries in the UK, Italy, Switzerland, Thailand, North America, New Zealand and Australia.

Ajahn Sumedho was born Robert Jackson in Seattle in the USA in 1934. Although brought up a Christian, he became more and more interested in the ideas and religion of the Far East. In 1963, he completed a doctorate in Far Eastern Studies and then decided to work as a teacher in Borneo.

Ajahn Sumedho

On a visit to Thailand in 1966, he decided to become an ordained monk of the order run by Ahajn Chah. In 1976, he was appointed the leader of the British **Sangha**.

Sumedho has written in his autobiography about the importance of Buddhist practice in helping him to understand how the world works. He wrote:

'The mind is like a mirror; it has the ability to reflect things. Mirrors reflect anything – beautiful or ugly, good or bad. And those things do not harm the mirror.'

In other words, we are not our own minds. He also wrote:

'We observe "This is how our lives have to be." Then we wisely use what we have, learn from it and free ourself from the narrow limits of self and mortality.'

A politician's story

In 1989, Aung San Suu Kyi was elected as the leader of Myanmar (Burma) by 80% of the voters.

Despite winning by such a large margin, the army stopped her from taking power by placing her under house arrest. They ruled that the election results did not count and that they were still in power. Aung San Suu Kyi had campaigned to remove corruption from the army and to make sure that all the people would not be abused by anyone in the army.

Her political party, the National League for Democracy, was banned. She was unable to leave the country, even when her husband died of cancer in her adopted country, the UK, in 1999.

Aung San Suu Kyi

As a Buddhist, Aung San Suu Kyi has told her party and her people that they must try to get the army to accept the result of the 1989 election by using non-violence. She had learnt from the example of the Hindu Indian leader, Mahatma Gandhi and the Christian civil rights leader, Martin Luther King. She has organized sit-ins and other protests in order to achieve peace and democracy.

Learning about religion

❶ What do you think might have attracted someone like Ajahn Sumedho to Buddhism?

❷ Do a search of the Internet to find references to Aung San Suu Kyi. You should be able to plan a wall display, outlining her life and beliefs.

❸ Write a speech for Aung San Suu Kyi (based on her Buddhist beliefs), urging her country to become a democracy.

Learning from religion

❶ Do you think non-violence can ever work against an oppressive government? Organize a class discussion on this topic. You will need to research examples from history such as Martin Luther King in the USA or Mahatma Gandhi in India to help you think about this.

❷ Find out more about Amnesty International and the work they do to protect human rights. Using their website, write a leaflet designed to introduce their work to someone your age.

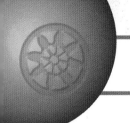

Glossary

Abidharma Pitaka this is the third of the three principal sections of the canon of basic scripture. It is a systematic, philosophical and psychological treatment of the teachings given in the Sutta Pitaka

Ahimsa pursuing harmlessness to all living creatures

Ananda the Buddha's successor in leading the Buddhist community

Ascesticism the belief that by punishing the body you will get to spiritual truth

Avalokitesvara a Bodhisattva representing perfect compassion

Bhikkhu fully ordained Buddhist monk

Bodh Gaya the place where Buddha became enlightened while sitting under the bodhi tree

Bodhisattva a being destined for enlightenment, who postpones final attainment of Buddhahood in order to help living beings

Brahma Viharas the four sublime states: loving kindness, compassion, sympathetic joy and evenness of mind

Buddha Awakened or Enlightened One

Buddhism the religion taught by the Buddha

Channa the chariot driver who took Siddhartha to the city and to the forest

Chunda the owner of the house where the Buddha ate what poisoned and killed him

Dalai Lama the spiritual and temporal leader of the Tibetan people

Dana generosity, giving, gift

Dharmapada famous scripture of 423 verses

Dharma the Buddha's teaching. Dharma means 'universal truth'

Dhyana concentration

Eightfold Path steps to be followed to reach nirvana, as suggested by the Buddha. They will lead to freedom from the idea of the self

Engaged Buddhism the idea that Buddhism should engage with the political and social questions of the world

Enlightenment experience of understanding what is true and what is not, to find the path

Five Moral Precepts five moral intentions that Buddhists try to live their lives by

Four Noble Truths the teaching of the Buddha on suffering, its causes and its solutions

Jataka the tales told of the Buddha's many rebirths

Karma intentional actions that affect one's circumstances in this and future lives. The Buddha's insistence that the effect depends on volition marks the Buddhist treatment of karma as different from the Hindu understanding of karma

Karuna compassion

Kisagami a female follower of the Buddha, believed by many to have formed an order of Buddhist nuns

Kshanti patience

Kusingara the place where the Buddha died

Lotus flower symbol of enlightenment

Lotus sutra key teaching of the Buddha

Lumbini Grove the place where according to legend the Buddha was born

Mahayana Buddhism one of the two main branches of Buddhism. Stresses the importance of Bodhisattvas

Maitreya a Bodhisattva who will bring a golden age in the future

Mala beads a string of 108 beads used to help meditation by some Buddhists

Mandalas images often made of sand to help Buddhists realize the changing nature of life

Mara a devil-like figure who tried to confuse Siddhartha in order to try to stop him becoming the Buddha

Meditation thinking deeply for religious reasons. Mental practice designed to help achieve enlightenment

Merit a deed that adds to good karma

Metta loving kindness

Middle Way the Buddha's teaching that the balance between pleasure and pain, the balance in life is necessary to achieve the way to enlightenment

Mudita sympathetic joy

Nagasena Buddhist thinker who compared the self to a chariot

Nirvana blowing out of the fires of greed, hatred and ignorance, the state of secure perfect peace that follows. A key Buddhist term

Obon Japanese Buddhist festival remembering the dead

Pagoda (Dagoda) Buddhist religious building designed on five levels to show the nature of the universe being made of five elements

Pali Canon the collected scriptures of Buddhism

Parinirvana the state of bliss entered into by the Buddha on his death

Pitaka 'basket', collection of scriptures

Prajna wisdom

Purowa platform that Buddhist couples stand on during marriage

Rahula son of Siddhartha Gautama. His name means 'chain'

Rupa an image of the Buddha

Samanera Buddhist novice monk

Sangha community, assembly. Often used for the order of bhikkus and bhikkunis in Theravadin communities. In the Mahayana countries, the Sangha includes lay devotees and priests, e.g. in Japan

Sarnath the place where, in the Deer Park, Buddha delivered his first sermon after being enlightened

Siddhartha Gautama the personal name of the historical Buddha

Sila morality

Skilful/Unskilful Buddhists talk about moral action in terms of skilful (right) and unskilful (inappropriate or wrong)

Songkran the Thai Buddhist new year festival

Stupa a Buddhist religious building which contains a sacred relic of the Buddha or an important Buddhist

Sutra Pitaka the second of the three collections – principally of teachings – that comprise the canon of basic scripture

Tara a Bodhisattva who helps in enlightenment

Theravada 'way of the elders', a principal school of Buddhism, established in Sri Lanka and South East Asia. Also found in the West

Three Refugees the three most important things in Buddhism: the Buddha, the Dharma (teaching) and the Sangha (the Buddhist community)

Tripitaka 'three baskets', a threefold collection of texts (Vinaya, Sutra, Abhidharma)

Upekkah serenity

Vihara dwelling place, monastery

Vinaya Pitaka the first of the three collections of the canon of basic scripture, containing mostly the discipline for monks and nuns, with many stories and some teachings

Viriya intention directed towards doing good

Wat name for a Buddhist temple in Thailand

Wesak Buddha Day. Name of a festival and a month. On the full moon of Wesak (in May or June), the birth, enlightenment and passing away of the Buddha took place, although some Buddhists celebrate only the birth at this time, e.g. Zen

Wheel of life symbol used to explain how humans are trapped into suffering by existence. Often shown with eight spokes, to show that following the Eightfold Path will help people escape from this life cycle

Yashodahra wife of Siddhartha Gautama

Index